Labrador Retriever PUPPIES

PUPPY PALS

by David and Patricia Armentrout

A Crabtree Seedlings Book

TABLE OF CONTENTS

CRABTREE
Publishing Company
www.crabtreebooks.com

School-to-Home Support for Caregivers and Teachers

This book helps children grow by letting them practice reading. Here are a few guiding questions to help the reader with building his or her comprehension skills. Possible answers appear here in red.

Before Reading:

• What do I think this book is about?
  • *I think this book is about Labrador retriever puppies.*
  • *I think this book is about how Labrador retriever puppies are friendly.*

• What do I want to learn about this topic?
  • *I want to learn if a Labrador retriever puppy would be a good pet.*
  • *I want to know if Labrador retriever puppies can swim.*

During Reading:

• I wonder why...
  • *I wonder why Labrador retrievers like to swim.*
  • *I wonder how they keep warm in cold water.*

• What have I learned so far?
  • *I have learned that Labrador retrievers make good family pets.*
  • *I have learned that puppies drink milk from their mother.*

After Reading:

• What details did I learn about this topic?
  • *I have learned that Labrador retrievers are brown, yellow, or black.*
  • *I have learned that Labrador retrievers like to fetch.*

• Read the book again and look for the vocabulary words.
  • *I see the word litter on page 5, and the word retrievers on page 13. The other glossary words are found on pages 22 and 23.*

Labrador Retriever Puppies

A **lab puppy** can be your best pal.

Lab moms have four to ten puppies in a **litter**.

The puppies drink milk from their mom.

Lab puppies are brown, yellow, or black.

They love to run and **fetch**.

That's why they are called **retrievers!**

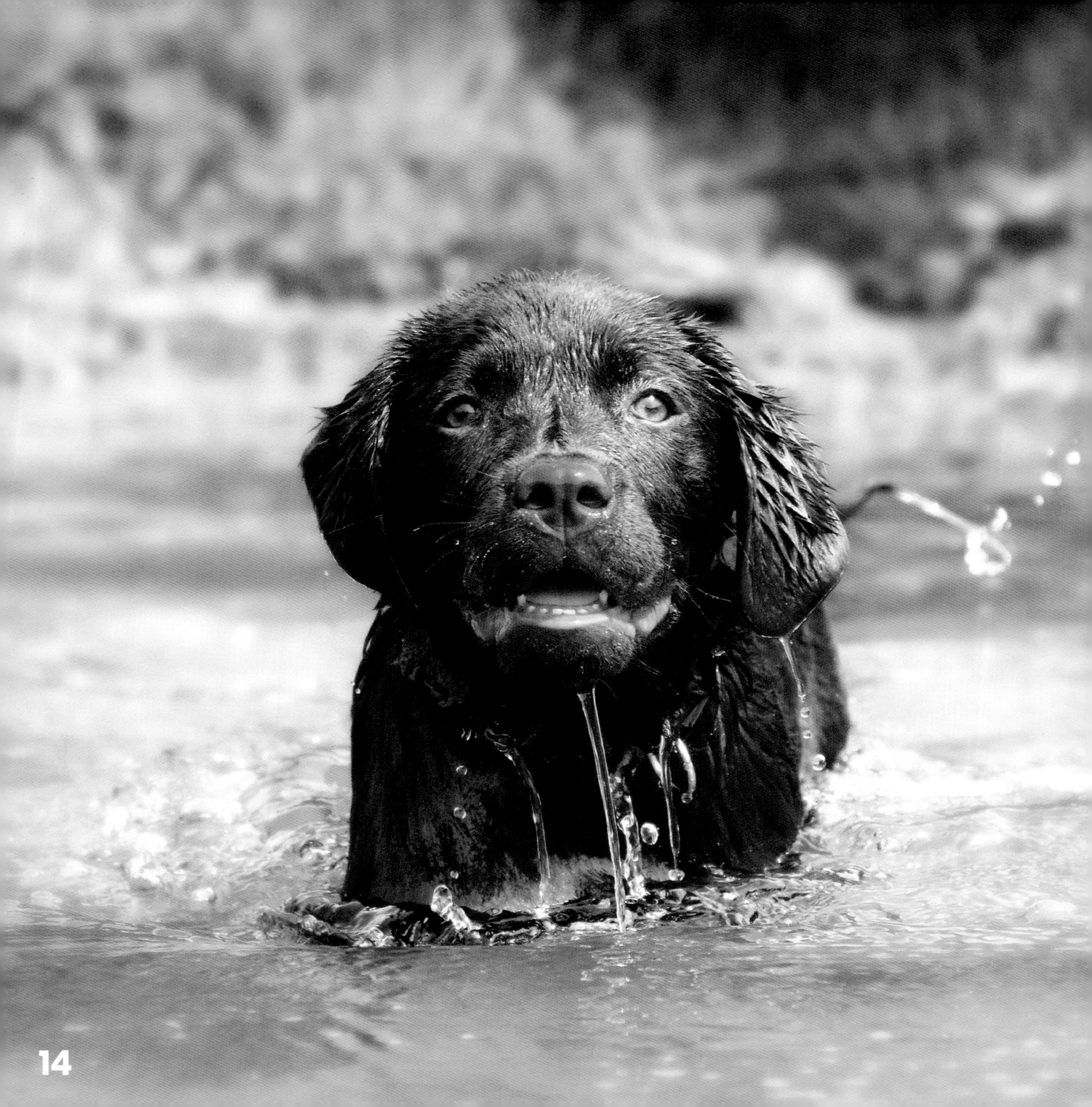

It's hard to keep a lab out of the water.

Thick **fur** keeps them warm in cold water.

Lab puppies grow up
to be big, lovable dogs!

They love to be part of the family.

Glossary

fetch (fech): Fetch means to go after and bring back something.

fur (fur): Fur is the soft, thick, hairy coat of an animal.

lab (lab): Lab is short for Labrador retriever.

litter (LIT-ur): A litter is a group of puppies or other animals born at the same time to one mother.

puppy (PUHP-ee): A puppy is a young dog.

retrievers (ri-TREE-vurz): Retrievers are certain kinds of dogs that can be trained to find and bring back things.

Index

Websites

https://www.akc.org/dog-breeds/best-dogs-for-kids/
https://www.goodhousekeeping.com/life/pets/g5138/best-family-dogs/

About the Authors

David and Patricia Armentrout
David and Patricia spend as much time as possible playing and caring for Gimli, Artie, and Scarlet, three special family dogs.

Photo Credits: Cover: photo shutterstock.com/Eric Isselee, background art shutterstock.com/Dream2designers. Title page: ©Shutterstock.com/Natalia Fedosova, page 3 ©Shutterstock.com/Nina Buday, page 4 ©Shutterstock.com/VSM Fotografia, page 6 ©Shutterstock.com/Oksana Mala, Page 8 ©Shutterstock.com/Natalia Fedosova, page 10 ©Shutterstock.com/ataglier, page 12 ©Shutterstock.com/Steve Oehlenschlager, page 14 ©Shutterstock.com/ mo30photography page 16 ©Shutterstock.com/maryo, page 18 ©Shutterstock.com/ Anna Tronova, page 20 ©Shutterstock.com/LightField Studios.

Library and Archives Canada Cataloguing in Publication

Title: Labrador retriever puppies / by David and Patricia Armentrout.
Names: Armentrout, David, 1962- author. | Armentrout, Patricia, 1960- author.
Description: Series statement: Puppy pals | "A Crabtree seedlings book". | Includes index.
Identifiers: Canadiana (print) 20210190949 | Canadiana (ebook) 20210190957 |
ISBN 9781427157706 (hardcover) |
ISBN 9781427157713 (softcover) |
ISBN 9781427157720 (HTML) |
ISBN 9781427157737 (EPUB) |
ISBN 9781427157744 (read-along ebook)
Subjects: LCSH: Labrador retriever—Juvenile literature. | LCSH: Puppies—Juvenile literature.
Classification: LCC SF429.L3 A76 2022 | DDC j636.752/7—dc23

Library of Congress Cataloging-in-Publication Data

Names: Armentrout, David, 1962- author. | Armentrout, Patricia, 1960- author.
Title: Labrador retriever puppies / David Armentrout, Patricia Armentrout.
Description: New York : Crabtree Publishing, 2022. |
Series: Puppy pals - a Crabtree seedlings book | Includes index.
Identifiers: LCCN 20210172O5 (print) | LCCN 20210172O6 (ebook) |
ISBN 9781427157706 (hardcover) |
ISBN 9781427157713 (paperback) |
ISBN 9781427157720 (ebook) |
ISBN 9781427157737 (epub) | ISBN 9781427157744
Subjects: LCSH: Labrador retriever—Juvenile literature. | Puppies—Juvenile literature
Classification: LCC SF429.L3 A76 2022 (print) | LCC SF429.L3 (ebook) |
DDC 636.752/7—dc23
LC record available at https://lccn.loc.gov/2021017205
LC ebook record available at https://lccn.loc.gov/2021017206

Written by: David and Patricia Armentrout
Designed by: Jennifer Dydyk
Editor: Kelli Hicks
Proofreader: Crystal Sikkens

Crabtree Publishing Company

www.crabtreebooks.com   1-800-387-7650

Printed in the U.S.A./062021/CG20210401

Published in the United States
Crabtree Publishing
347 Fifth Avenue, Suite 1402-145
New York, NY, 10016

Published in Canada
Crabtree Publishing
616 Welland Ave.
St. Catharines, Ontario L2M 5V6